You Are Hope

Elise Conroy

BookLeaf Publishing

Presentation by *BookLeaf Publishing*

Web: www.bookleafpub.com

E-mail: info@bookleafpub.com

ISBN: 9789395969659

First edition 2022

DEDICATION

To all those who have seen me in my darkest times and chosen to still love me and help me see myself as they do. And to those who will see you in yours.

ACKNOWLEDGEMENT

Those who deserve my thanks have received it. (And if you're unsure, let me know and I will be sure to thank you).

Thank you to you for giving me a chance to help and bring some light and hope.

PREFACE

In some of my darkest times, stories have helped me to feel more connected to the world. However, in my absolute lowest days, I couldn't focus on those stories or even long poems. I challenged myself to write a poem every day for a month (spoiler alert: I didn't succeed, but I did keep writing at random times and have a number of poems now). Having a short, poetic form to stick to was helpful and challenging and made me feel like I accomplished something when I desperately needed to feel that I was contributing.

This is a collection of haikus - 3 line poems - that I hope you can turn to when you most need something small and quick to connect with. Whether it's wanting to know you aren't alone in your feelings, wanting to remember that hope is important and hard and scary sometimes, or wanting to give yourself a little dose of hopeful encouragement.

This is my small contribution to you. A sampling of the poems that I have written in times when I needed to feel productive, like I still existed even in the dark, and that I wasn't alone. I hope you find a bit of hope in them as well and use them as you need to.

Shadows

There are no shadows
When plunged so deep in darkness
Because there's no light

Flowers

The flowers still bloom
But soon they will wither dead
Leaving emptiness

Light

There is no light here
In this place I’ve been so long
There is no comfort

Life

Taking back my life
Is the most impossible task
In this great big mess

Tunnel

It just seems endless
This tunnel I've been stuck in
For way too long now

Tunnel

The tunnel is long
But there is light at the end
Keep moving onward

Healing

My body is weak
I’m tired and defeated
My soul wants healing

Comsumption

The dark consumes me
Still a tiny spot of light
Tries to get through

Grief

Trying hard to hope
It seems to be my default
But grief keeps me down

Starlight

Look for starlight
When the darkness consumes you
It will give you hope

Good

Feel all of it through
No matter how much it hurts
Good will come again

Reason

There is a reason
Even when you can’t see it
And want to let go

Frozen

Life won’t ever stop
Even when you feel frozen
In a single spot

Invisible

Not invisible
Just because they don't see you
You are still right here

Together

Beautiful sunrise
And the deepest, densest fog
Exist together

Reminder

Needed reminders:
The birds chirp and the world turns
Even in the cold

Eternal

Hope springs eternal
Better days are on the way
Stay here to get there

Focus

Focus on today
Just try to find your reason
For this one moment

Little

It’s in little things
Where hope lies and waits for you
Don’t miss out on them

Truth

For you and for me
We are worthy of this life
That’s the truest truth

Hope

Hope is inside you
Though you don't want to hear it
You will be okay

www.ingramcontent.com/pod-product-compliance
Lightning Source LLC
Chambersburg PA
CBHW062111140826
49812CB00058B/1252
9789395969659